DINOSAURS!

DINOSAURS!

A Drawing Book by Michael Emberley

Little, Brown and Company

Boston   Toronto   London

First Edition

Library of Congress Cataloging in Publication Data

Emberley, Michael.
   Dinosaurs!

   SUMMARY: Presents instructions for drawing a
variety of dinosaurs.
      1. Dinosauria in art—Juvenile literature.
   2. Extinct animals in art—Juvenile literature.
   3. Animal painting and illustration.   [1. Dinosaurs
in art.   2. Drawing—Technique]   1. Title.
   NC780.5.E4   743'.6   79-24379
   ISBN 0-316-23417-6 (hardcover)
   ISBN 0-316-23631-4 (paperback)

HC: 10   9
PB: 10   9   8   7   6   5

                              H

*Published simultaneously in Canada
by Little, Brown & Company (Canada) Limited*

PRINTED IN THE UNITED STATES OF AMERICA

To Papa

What, Where, How,

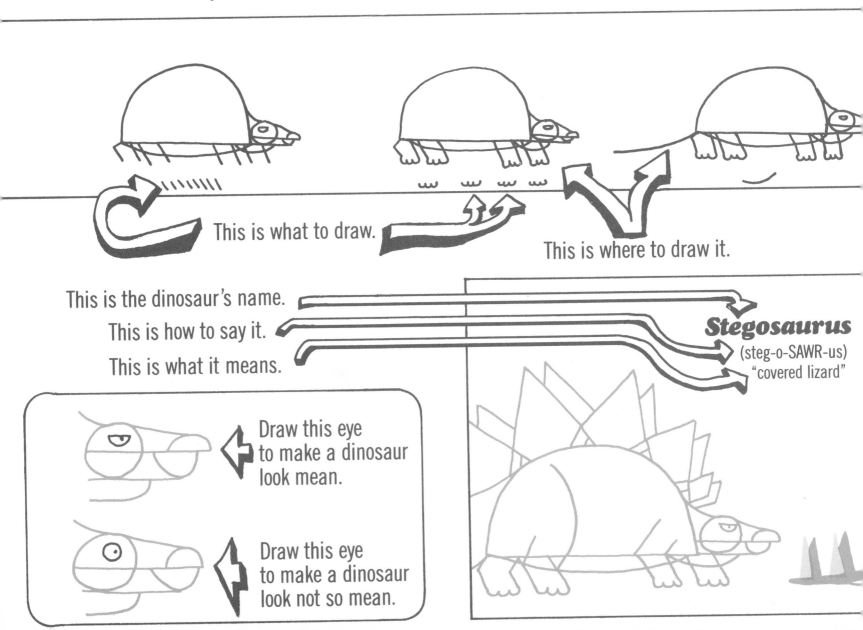

This is what to draw.

This is where to draw it.

This is the dinosaur's name.

This is how to say it.

This is what it means.

Stegosaurus
(steg-o-SAWR-us)
"covered lizard"

Draw this eye to make a dinosaur look mean.

Draw this eye to make a dinosaur look not so mean.

Etc.

Since no one has ever seen a living dinosaur, you can color them any way you like.

To make things like legs and fins really look like they are behind something, just color them a little darker.

The word dinosaur (DINE-o-sawr) means "terrible lizard." However, not all dinosaurs were so terrible, nor were they actually lizards. In fact, three of the animals in this book are not really dinosaurs, they are other types of prehistoric animals: Ichthyosaurus is a type of swimming reptile called an ichthyosaur; Pteranodon is a type of flying reptile called a pterosaur; and Dimetrodon is an earlier reptile who was an ancestor of the dinosaurs and died out before the dinosaurs emerged.

Dimetrodon

(dye-MET-ro-don)

"two sizes of teeth"

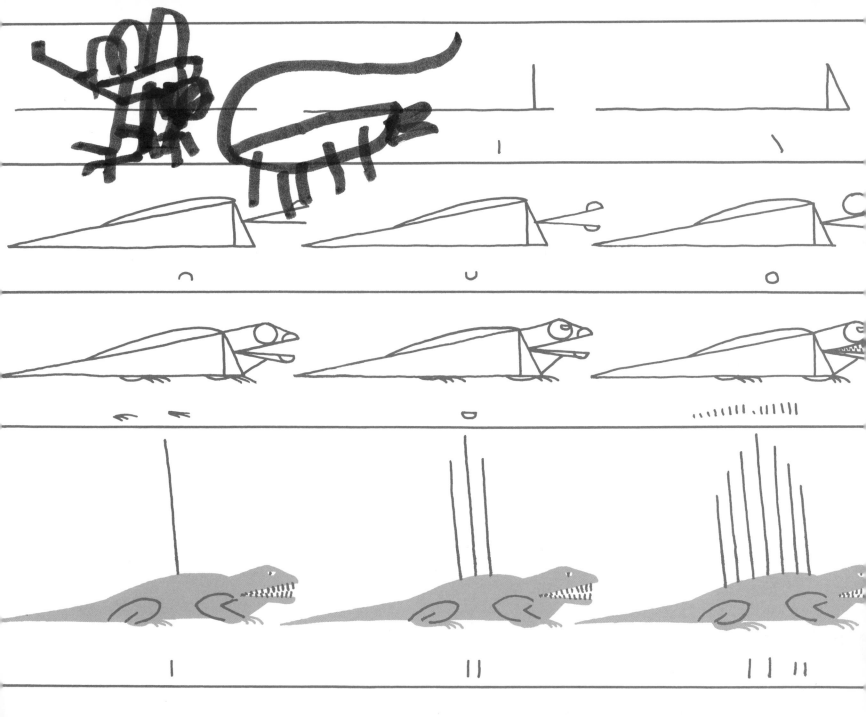

Brachiosaurus

(brak-ee-o-SAWR-us)

"great-arms lizard"

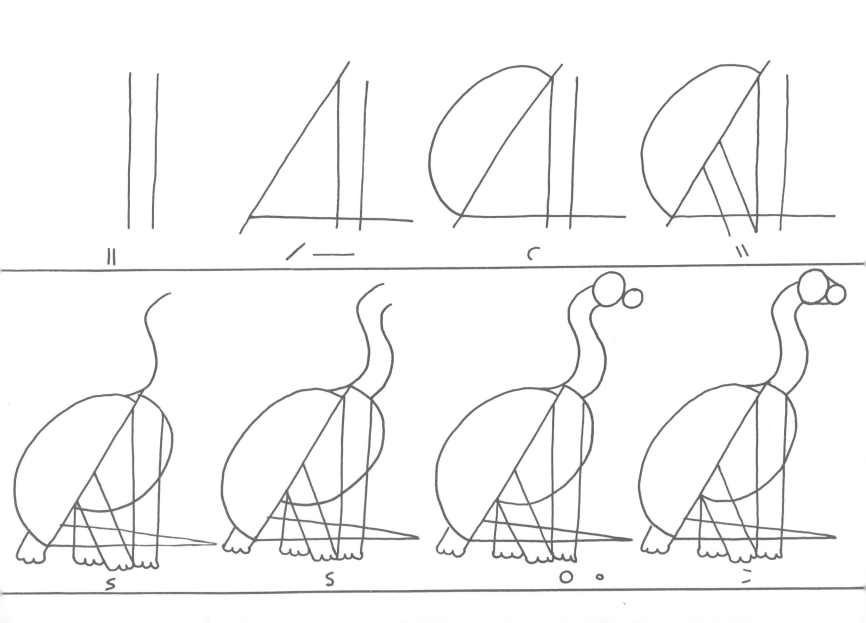

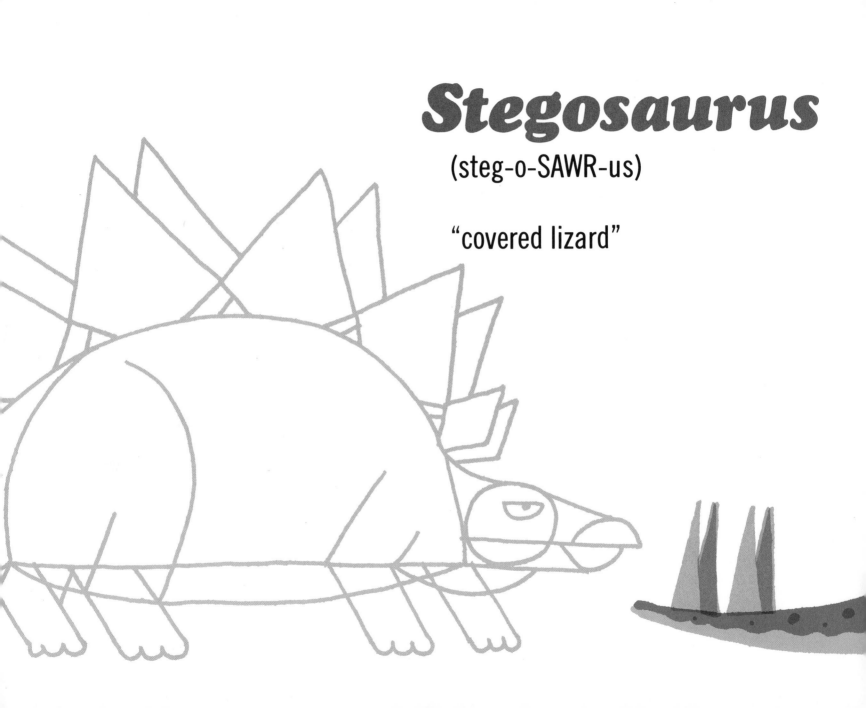

Stegosaurus

(steg-o-SAWR-us)

"covered lizard"

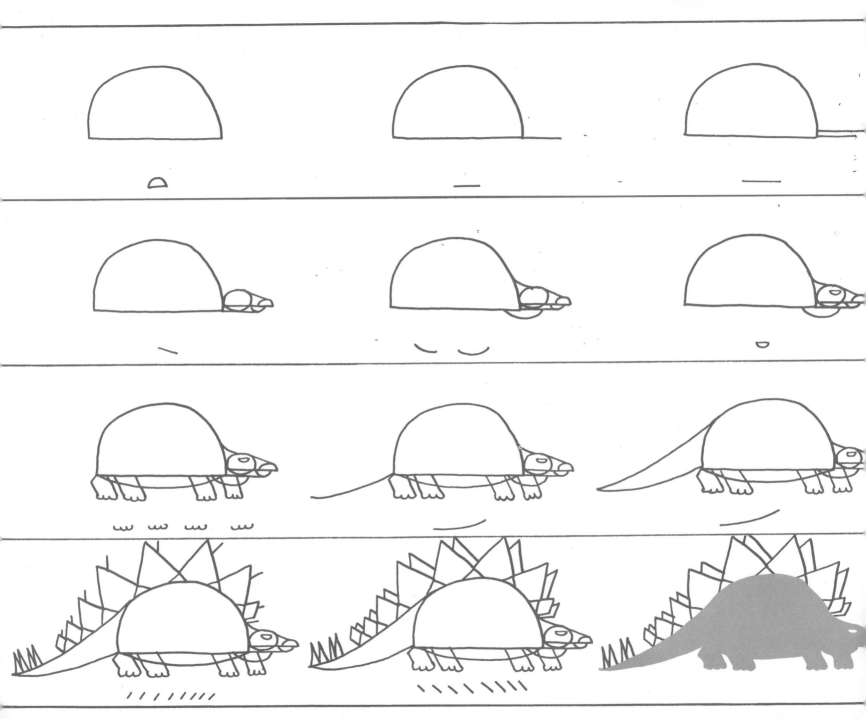

Kentrosaurus

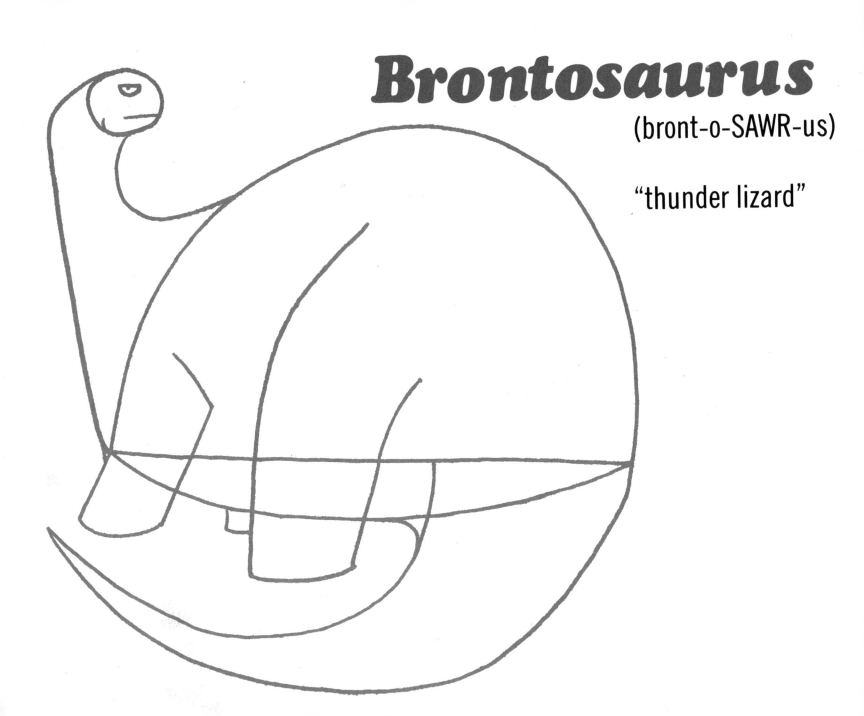

Brontosaurus

(bront-o-SAWR-us)

"thunder lizard"

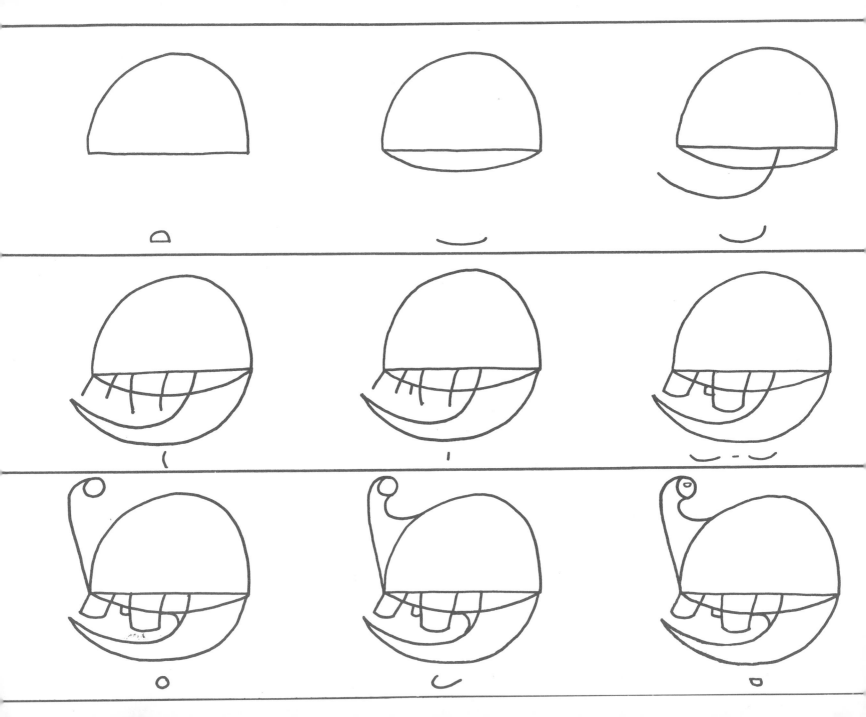

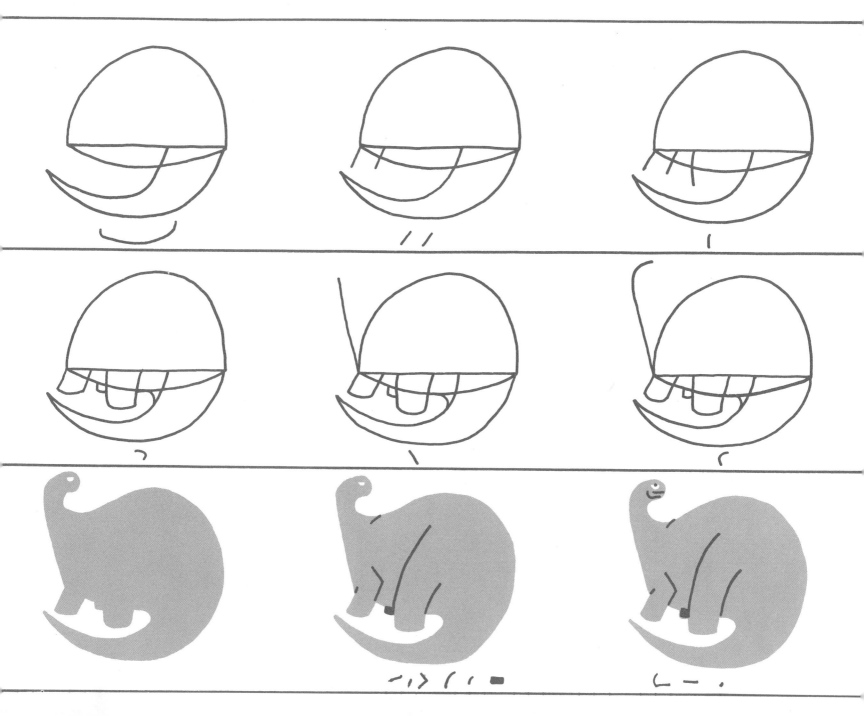

Ornitholestes

(orn-i-tho-LESS-teez)

"bird stealer"

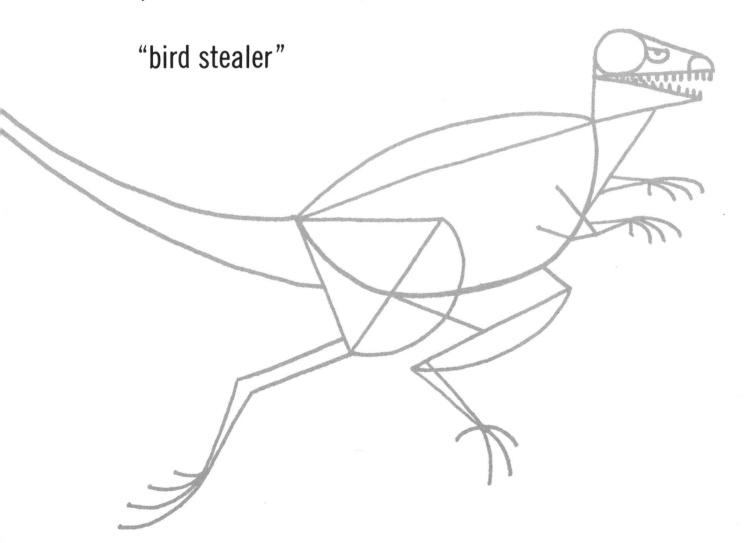

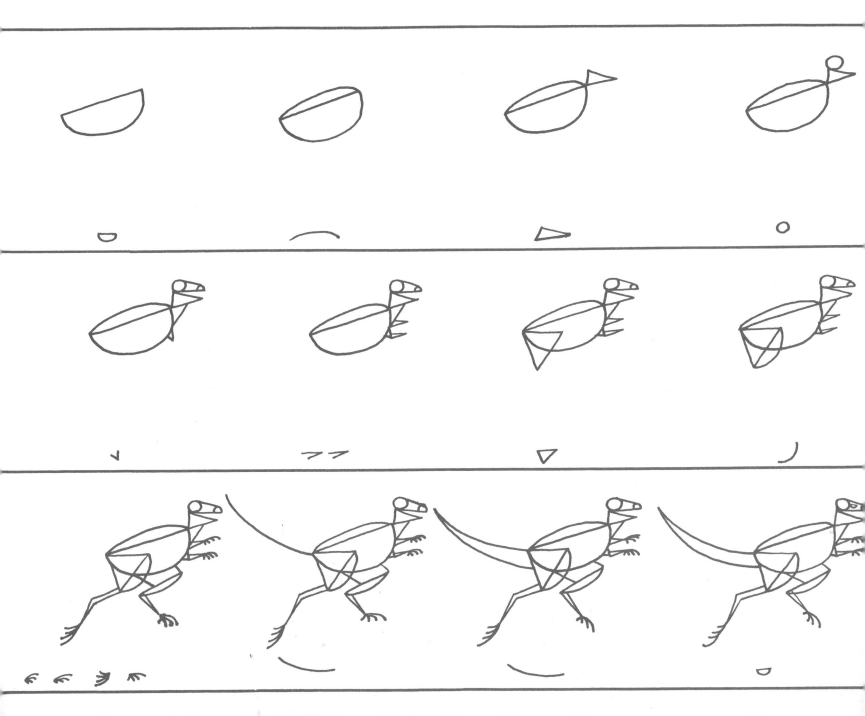

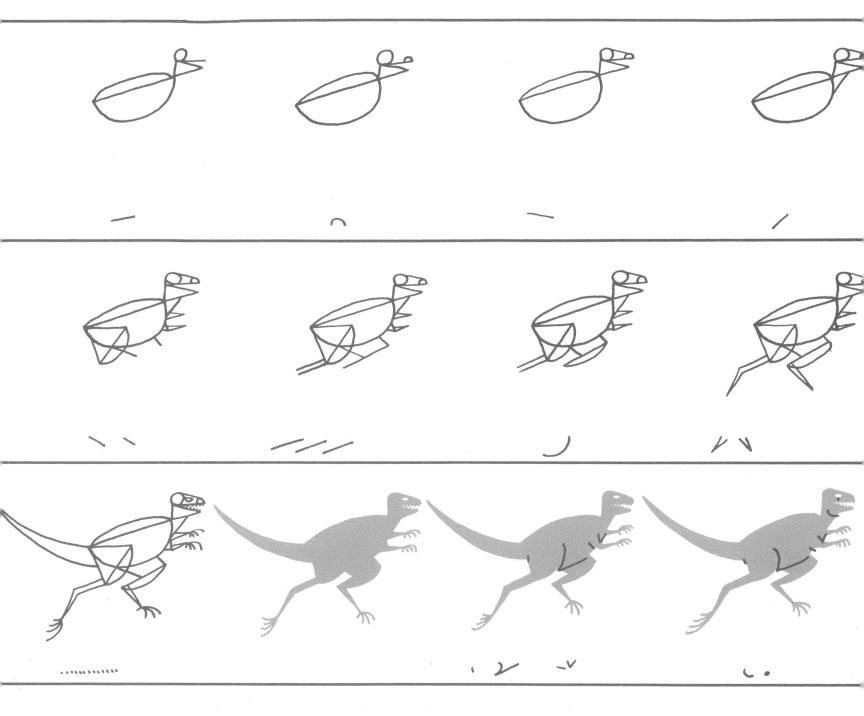

Iguanodon

(i-GWAN-o-don)

"iguana tooth"

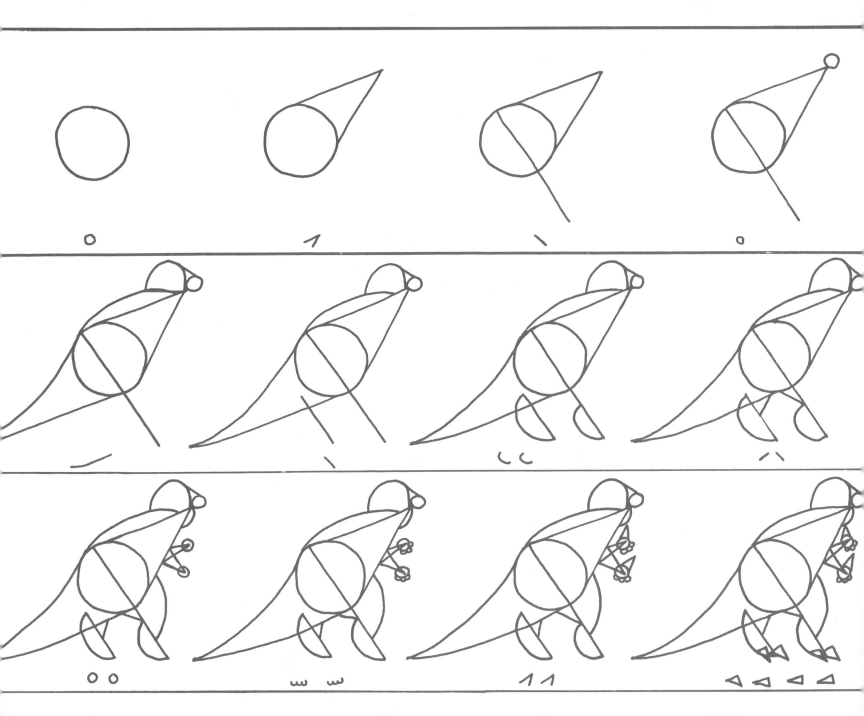

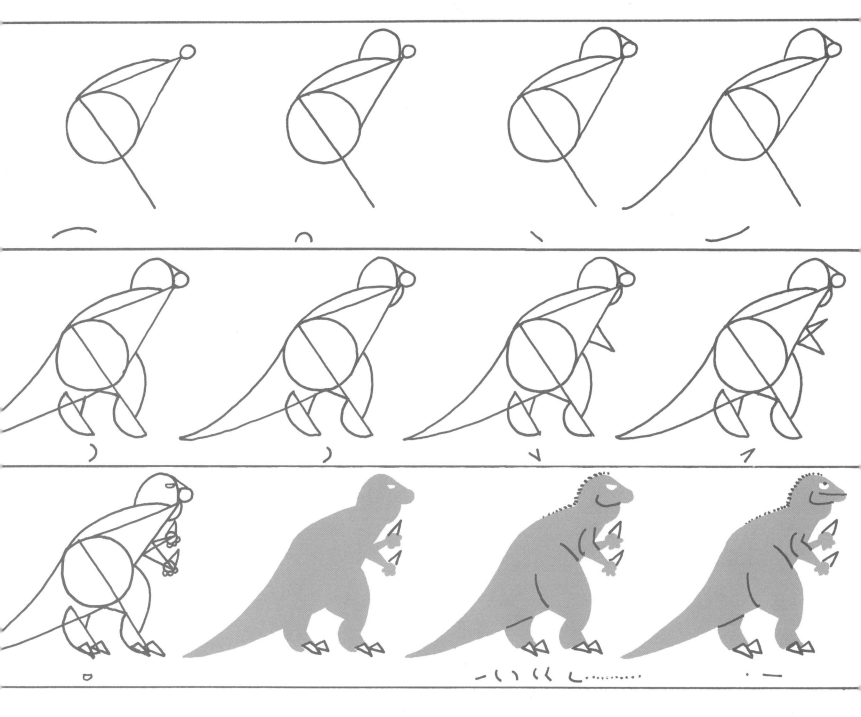

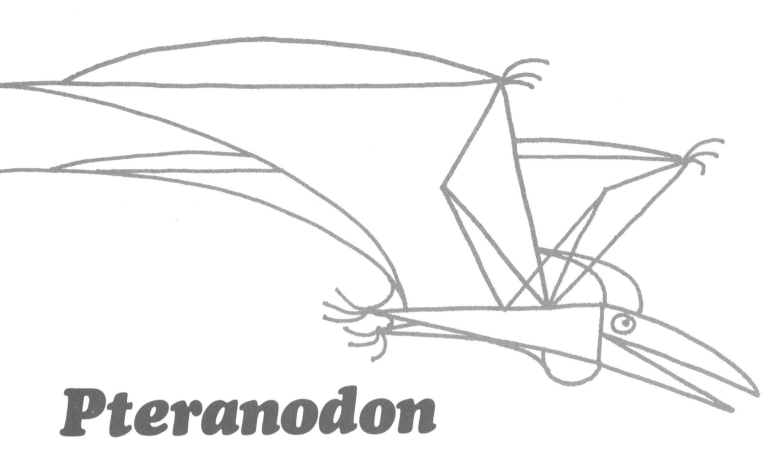

Pteranodon

(ter-AN-o-don)

"toothless wing"

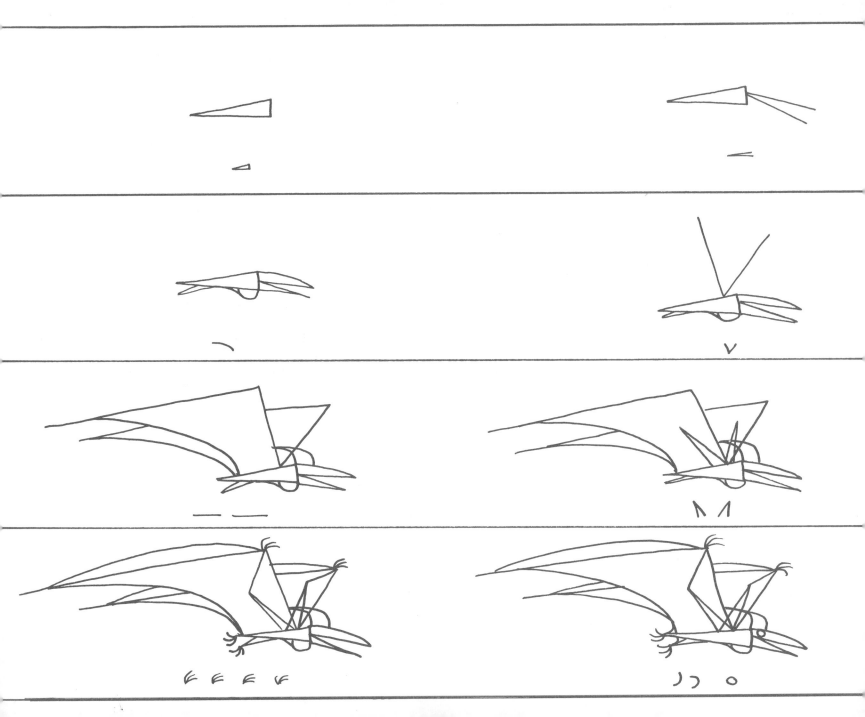

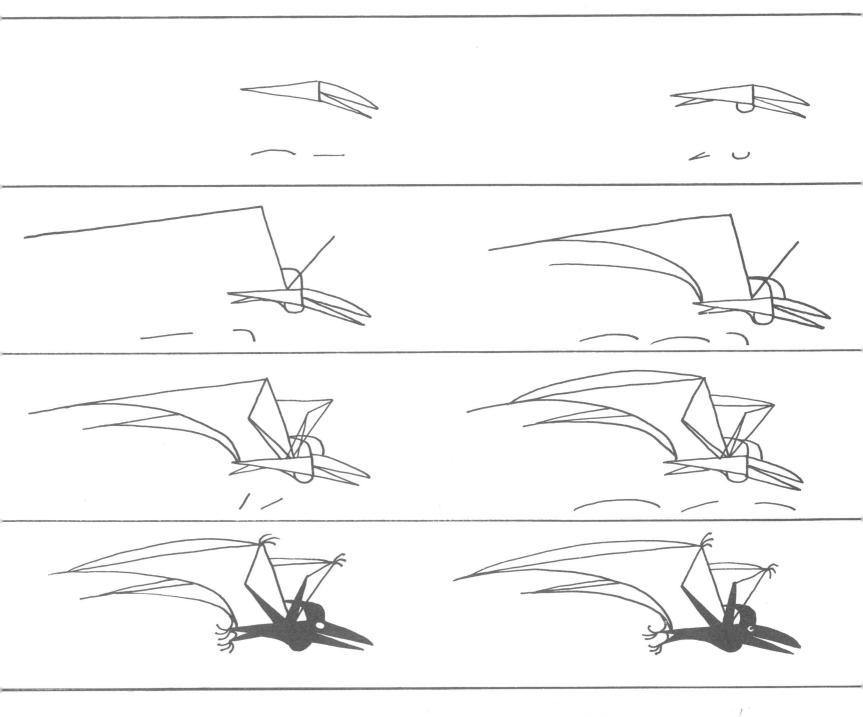

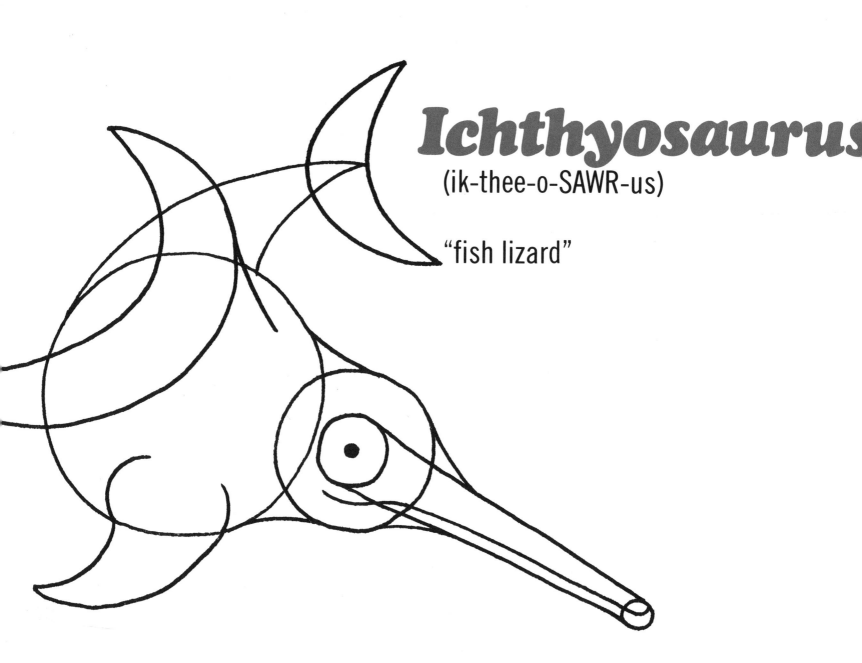

Ichthyosaurus

(ik-thee-o-SAWR-us)

"fish lizard"

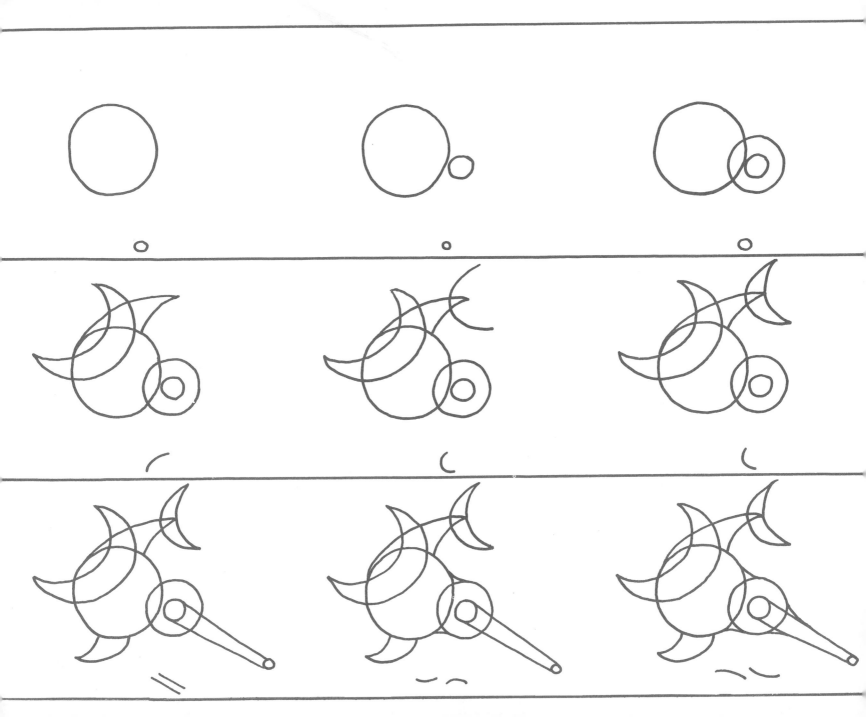

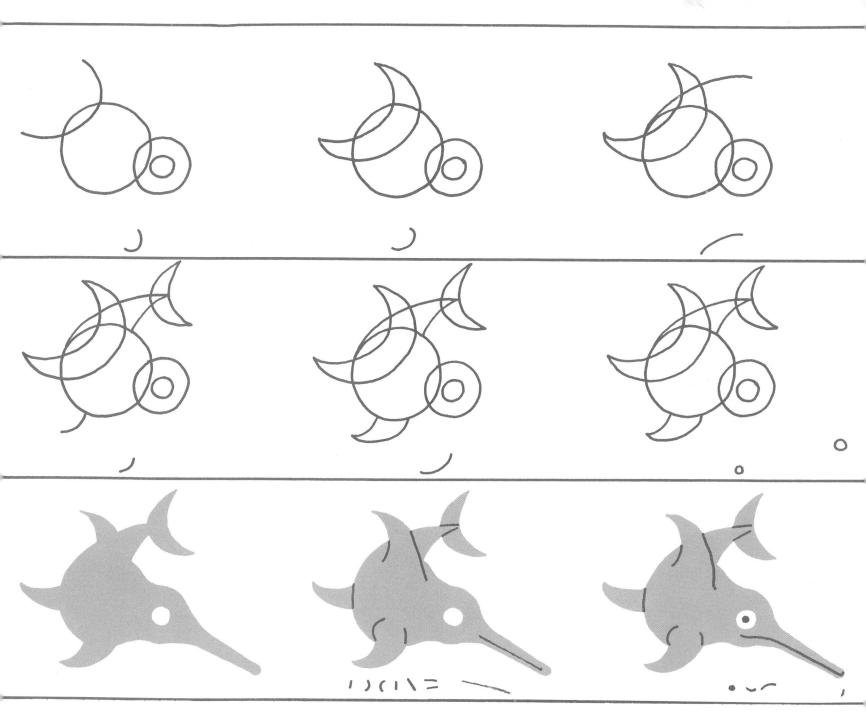

Triceratops

(try-SER-a-tops)

"three-horned face"

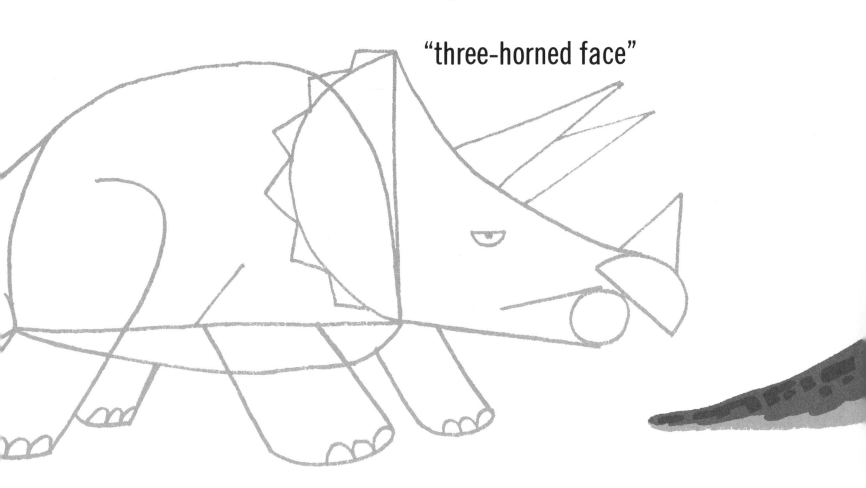

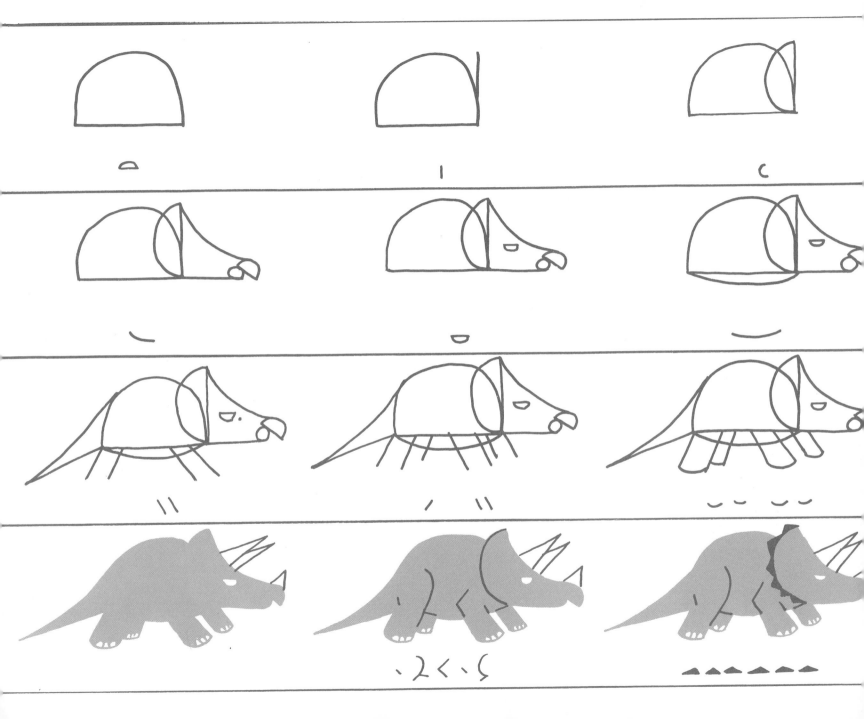

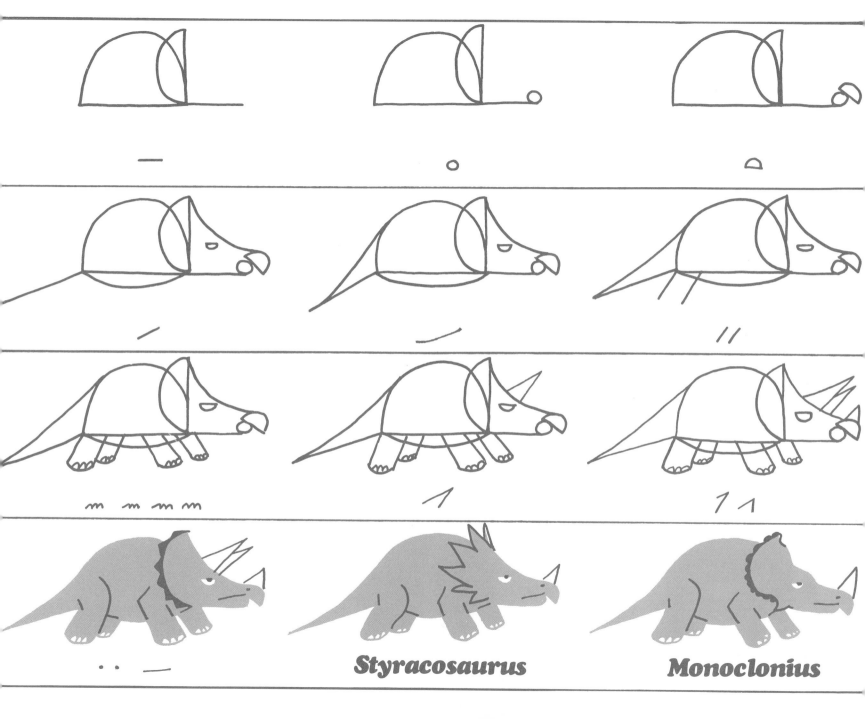

Styracosaurus

Monoclonius

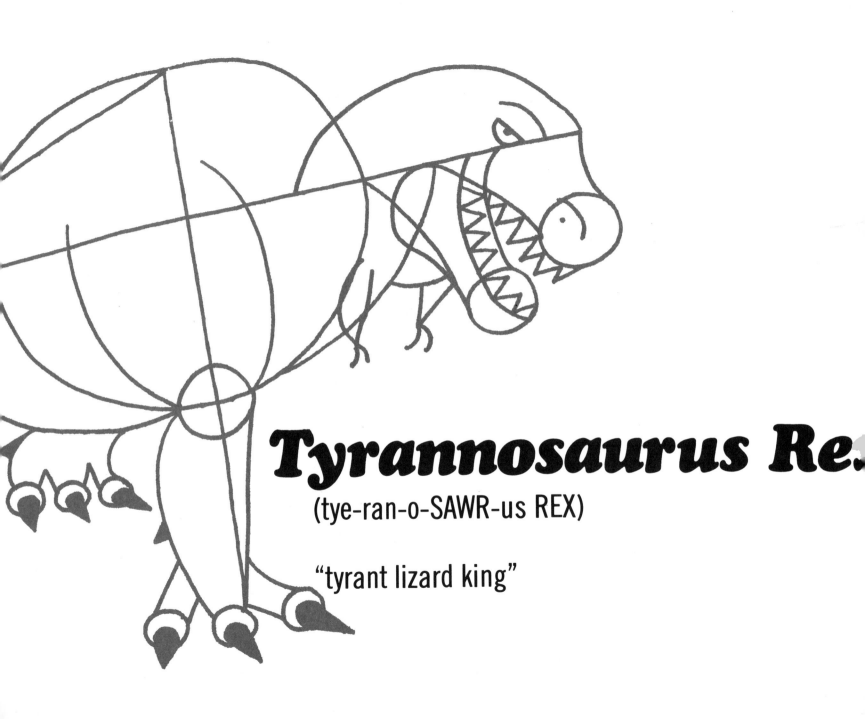

Tyrannosaurus Rex

(tye-ran-o-SAWR-us REX)

"tyrant lizard king"

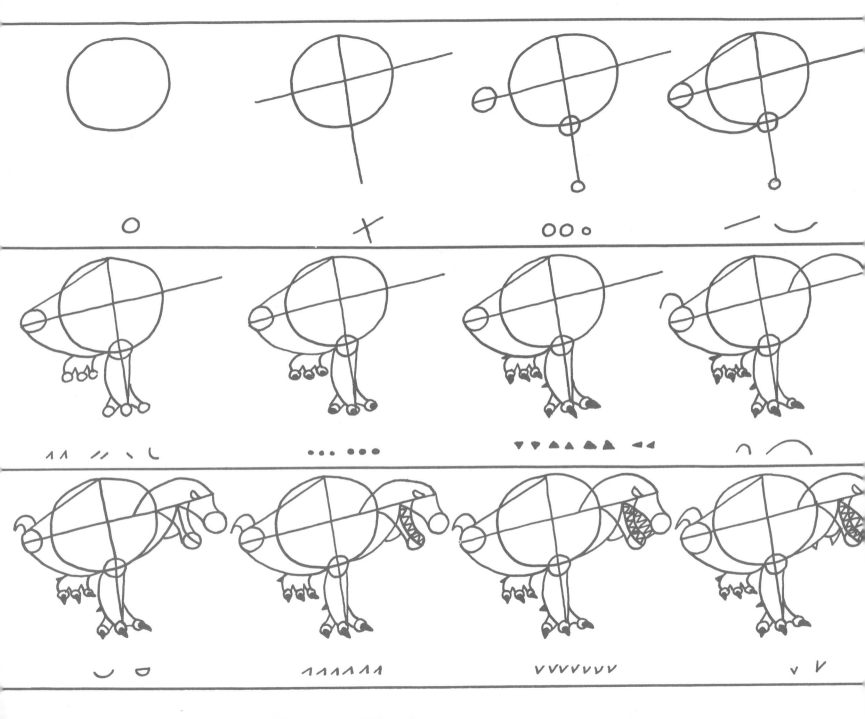

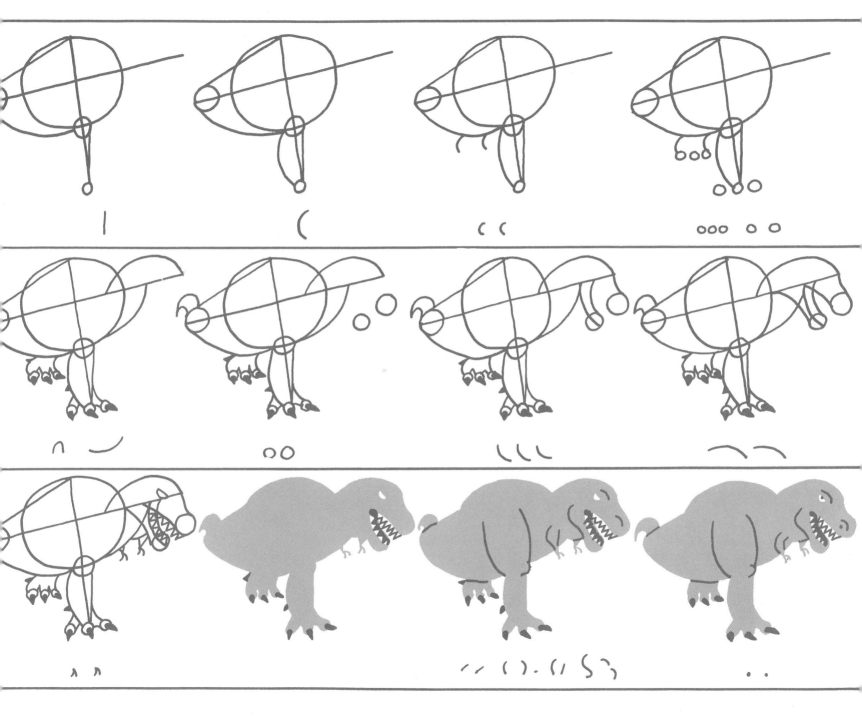

Here is how the sizes of the dinosaurs in this book would compare if they stood next to each other. They wouldn't have been able to stand next to each other, however, because they did not all live during the same time period.